40

poems found in the desert.

Richard Rayner

DEDICATION

These thoughts, reflections and expressions are written with sincere thanks to those people who have ever had the courage, honesty, compassion and love to speak intentional words to me.

Words from the pulpit, words across a beer or fractured sentences at the right time, they all are the tools and shadow of a Greater Poet for which I am grateful.

CONTENTS

Good news

The Word

Not a book of rules about seniority
Or the heavy hand of a leader's authority
But on every page an invitation
To every tongue and all the nations
To come join the great adventure
To leave the edge and join the center
To walk away from old and dying
To grab the truth stop the lying
To find in every moment peace
And to those in chains set free, release
Take hold and trust, and see and taste
Of God's great love for his human race.

The first romance

Would it have mattered, back in Eden
(If forbidden fruit had not been eaten
And creator God did not evict
The hiding couple who had been tricked)
Whom you married?

Would perfection have made us all the same
With equal good, but different names
And how would you differentiate
On what grounds would you find a mate
Whom you married?

If all were good and selfless men
On each you really could depend
With every maid kind and honest too
How could you find the one for you
Whom you married?

Something about our personality
Would have drawn us close, brought you to me
There must have been some fine romance
Rather than leave it all to chance
Whom you married

And so now banished it seems to me
It still remains a mystery
I'm blessed by God and cursed by none
To find myself to be the one
Whom you married

A clerihew for Moses

What a quandary you've set us Moses
The law you wrote contention poses
Rules to obey that highlight sin
Yet points the way to life within

Psalm 1

See him go, that wicked man
Walking briskly
Keeping pace
Standing in the wrong place.

See him sit, that mocking man
Other's reputation
He disturbs
Then recreates, with his words.

See him delight, the meditative man
Streamside tree
Taking rest
In the chair of obedience.

See him planted, the evergreen man
Providing shelter
In all seasons
To those who need it.

See the stream, flowing smoothly
Feeding sons
Feeding daughters
By tree with roots near living waters.

To the psalmist and his God

Yes! I know Him too!
Psalmist, and I too have poured out my frustration
And tears
And joys
And thanksgiving to Him.
I have read about Him in the Gospels
This God found in the desert
You and I are friends with much in common
And I would love to embrace you.

Yahweh see this man
Draw near to him and hear him
As he pours out his real life to you
Love him
Comfort him
Rescue him
As I know that is who you are.
He is my brother
And I stand beside him
And all those whose hearts ring then resonate
With petitions to your almighty goodness.

And to the both of you
I find myself honestly trite and unworthy
Made comfortable by both companion and compassion
Knowing others have stood where I stand
Knelt where I kneel
Prayed where I pray
Wept where I wept
Repented where I repent.
To find you have washed my face with my tears
Fed me with my laughter
And hollowed me out with your pen.

Nativity

A thousand colours bright and resplendent
Surround the sovereign on his throne
And voices crying God most holy
Echo and thunder in Heaven's home.

Whilst angels watch with awe and wonder
And bended knee and low bowed head
A love that knows no bounds or limits
Lays this aside, for a straw filled bed.

Now satisfied by maiden's breast
And rested well, he wakes to cry.
To silence claims that God is dead
For he is very much alive.

A tenacious love

I am returning home from far away
With weak knees
And complaining feet whose insistent voice is inaudible next to a
deafening heart
Whose sorrow echoes within its chambers then resonates
throughout my entire mind and body

I may not survive this journey's toll
But just let me get home first
To end my days forgiven
And complete my breath loved
In the house of my father
To expire on route would leave me forever estranged.

There is only one thing that gives my hope strength
And provides this sorrowful heart with the tenacity required to
make it home.
It is the great love of my father
That envelopes my cold shoulders like a thick blanket
And keeps me closer to him than the ring on his right hand, even
when I have been distant.
He cares for my tired, aching feet.
And fills our bellies with the calf optimistically fattened, should I
return.
He has been ready for my arrival for many days and weeks and
months and years.

But I have no need for robes, rings and revelry
Generous expressions of his joy
All I really want is to sit and talk
To listen to his gentle tones, lilting phrasing
As he calmly chooses the perfect words for me to hear.
Because he knows me.

A jar unbroken

Here and now, in this moment, let me not miss this favorable
exchange
Of a jar smashed for a body broken,
Moisturising balm for cuts and bruising,
An exchange making me rich beyond my wildest dreams.
So that those with me will not always be poor
Because I will have treasures to share.

Mary has taken the best thing she has and like herself,
Broken and contents poured out,
Offered it in front of everyone.
In exchange she has become what she valued,
A coin with your image and writing upon it,
your eternal treasure.
Being made famous, an example to all.

Whilst I, like Judas, remain unbroken,
Reserved, safe and capable
Denying all in the house the fragrance of my perfume.
Unchanging from costly man made coins,
that thief may steal and nature corrode.
My own eternal companion.
Becoming infamous and a warning to all.

The kiss

What kind of message could he send
What kind of invention could be created
Or metaphor applied
That would demonstrate His desire to
Draw us close and have us breathe His breath
Smell is clothes and feel his warmth
Surely there is no communication
Greater than the kiss.

And yet when his love is spurned
And another lover chosen
He takes this greatest of all devices
And demonstrates His desire to
Move closer to us and breathe our breath
Smell our clothes and feel our warmth
Surely there is no betrayal
Greater than a kiss.

A father's restraint

A father's ear called to attention
Immediately turned and tuned to the garden cry for help
A bee sting, stray dog or perhaps a fast bicycle accident.

Only one name on the lips of the child
As a vocal flare shoots into the evening sky
Voiced at certain pitch that sounds the alarm.

"Dad"

The core of all fatherly duties called into action
The defining obligation, parenting 101
To keep children safe and protect from harm.

But the garden crier receives no comfort
Never such parental restraint seen before or since
No bee sting, grazed knee or bent spoke to be found.

Just a cup.

A clerihew for the Messiah

Jesus Emmanuel
Took it ever so well
"A glutton and drunk who ritually stinks",
Placing our cup to his mouth, obediently drinks.

For the love of Pete

Why did the chicken cross the lake?
To be with Jesus.

Who do I think you are?
The Christ, the Messiah
The confession upon which your church will be built.

Not on me, fickle as the wind blown lake
One moment striding on water to meet you
The next scared of the tumultuous sea.
As unfaithful as the lover at dinner
Pretending not to know you the following morning,
And even after seeing the dead raise to life
I'm still afraid of upsetting the old guard.

And so I sit down with you
Once again having impetuously leapt from a boat.
Ashamed, embarrassed and in front of everyone a failure.
But I know only you have the words of life
Words that ask just one question.
"Do you love me?"

A clerihew for Peter

Less peripheral vision, Mr Peter
Would make your ocean walks much sweeter
And not being scared of another's opinion
Would save new converts from circumcision!

Paul's conversion

When religion dies and faith is born.

Stolen from right under the nose of darkness
The sword is turned into a plough.

The great reader and student groomed for a privileged position
Becomes the writer and explainer
Enabling and preparing others for great service.

The vigilant leader being taken by the hand
And led blind to the place where he would
Have the scales removed from His eyes
Able to see the world anew.

The soaring hawk, causing fear and panic
watched wherever he went by his prey.
Made invisible for 3 years and hidden
In land of shifting sand, motionless rock and burning sun.
Drinking life giving water from a new well.

The keeper of the gate and protector of the faith
Returning to the temple and declaring with a whole life made
whole
That the door is open and all may come in.
The hunter of people becomes a fisher of men,
The holder of coats becomes the giver of shirts,
The powerful and secure has become unwaveringly and boldly
vulnerable.

A clerihew for Paul

Paul of Tarsus
Would you not put it past us
Not to read a single letter
Though insights gained would make us better.

Being found

Clean plate

There was no gristle, rind or bitter stalk
Pushed aside when God's love consumed me.
Clean plate.

Trust

Darkness all around me
No matter how decrepit, evil or violent
Ever caused me fear.

That I reserve for the darkness within me.
That I fear like the silent shark
Stalking and unseen
Slipping through the unfathomable waters of my heart.
And so I swim, frantic,
To climb aboard your boat.
But you say stay in the water
And I shall keep you safe
I am the Lord, of all creation.

The goodness of God

Heaven overflows
My cup filled and spilling now
Quenches others thirst.

Eggs Calvary

What on earth would cause a man to put all his eggs into one basket?
Gratitude.

Build this temple

Words as stones from great aged quarry
Extract, reshape, transport, arrange
Piled high creating multi-storey
Polished temple, from rock estranged.

Within the rooms and lauded hallways
Rest great truths from men's great minds
Tested, proven through the ages
Museum pieces of great finds.

Standing back to view this wonder
Hands on hips, the good work done
The evening sun warms face and under
Bluest sky, the rest is won.

Viewing, basking, tripping, falling
On Stone not found, but which found me.
Surprising Rock which now is calling
To leave my temple of vanity.

I count as loss all prior intention
And put aside temple of mine
Now of this Stone, I only mention
When comprehending Rock divine.

Trade winds

Long, predictable, dependable, seasonal winds
That man can plan and prepare by,
Carrying spices and wine, stories and song, from land to land and
people to people.

Great vessels will be built to ride these nautical pathways
Hauling great treasures and amassing significant fortunes
As billowing sails reach out to, and join in with, the blowing
movement.

Small gusts that are here one moment and gone the next provide
Nothing but a short chill or a temporary nudge to a mariner
Already set in his course.

A temporary excitement to inflate the short sighted
Or cause a small child to wrap their coat tightly around
And bury their chin into their chest
And tighten their grip on parents hand.

And so I will trade winds.

Appearing

What my Grandmother taught me about the second coming of Christ

Standing by the galvanized barrier
waiting for her arrival,
best shorts on and shoes tied up.

Smells and sounds of numbered bus and coaches unloading their cargo,
spilling out onto other platforms
passengers who are of no interest to me.

My undistracted observation, waiting for bus of anticipated number
to arrive and stop at this platform.
Her arrival certified by the sight of her face,
Not looking for sweets, or gifts, but more than anything else to run
and embrace.

Whilst she talks to my mother
She holds my hand and gently squeezes.
The sweetest communion.

Bride's rapture

Take me not from earth's sweet smell
Of dusty trails and fresh water falling across stones made smooth
by centuries consistency.
Of pastures rich, swollen hillsides and familiar village green
Where sweet tone of music's sway animates the couples dance,
And for all our hardships, there is a soothing breeze.

Please, keep me here, in local life,
Where cathedrals, myth, history and family tell the story of divine
grace
And patience, kindness and forgiveness are pointed lights that
pierce night's dark shroud.
Stars as these may not shine so bright in another world where I
would miss them,
And I have come to love their celestial guidance.

So come to me, King in disguise, to lowly shepherdess.
To garden, mountaintop and lakeside you have already been
Did you not enjoy hospitable meals, desert tents arranged in
orderly fashion,
Secret evening visits to discuss things hidden and now revealed,
Our Friend in need and Friend indeed.

So if you have a choice,
If there is a balance in the matter that I can sway, please come and
visit, come and stay.
As the groom travels to the brides church and so to wed
So bring your household here, that you would be present, and I
would be with you.
Do not whisk me away.

Prophetic moon

The quiet night, cold and restrictive
Issues a fearful shudder upon seeing the prophetic moon, as it arcs
across the blackest of skies.

Set against this hour of darkness and the enshrouding cold and
damp
It is a lunar warning, to all that love the night,

Dawn will arrive

And an encouragement to all that love the day,
As the lightest touch of gossamer moonbeams dance on the water
and paddocks shine and sway in the nocturnal breeze under its
luminous glow.

This prophetic moon reflects to the earth what is now hidden, yet
will soon arrive with certainty.
Heralded by the joyful dawn chorus and resurrection of sleepers to
a new day.

Companion

Companion, with our masters bread
Come sit down with me and eat
Let us take our time
Sharing the same loaf

Let us mark this hour together
In simple familiarity
In talk and in silence
Until we rise.

Stories from the kingdom

The 8th day of creation

When all the day's work that can be done, has been done
And the children have been put to bed
And conversations with spouse have explored their winding paths
All my tasks, duties and loves are completed.

When the dog is already asleep, breathing shallowly and sprawled
upon her rug
And the chicken has found her roost for the night, quiet and still
And the only sound is some distant traffic, or quiet, muffled
plumbing.

I know I have some time with you
Between this moment and sleep
I can thank you for continuing your creation for one more day
And inviting me to join in your labour of love.

A prayer for my enemy

Oh how it burns
And spreads rapidly
This forest fire within my heart.
It wakes me in the night
And consumes my day.

This flaming hatred
That clouds my vision with its acrid smoke
Can be brought under control
If your great wind would blow
And fan the flames in the direction of my pride
And stubbornness.

Let it burn away my logical and informed self righteousness
And in its smouldering wake
Forge a path
Through which your blessings
Would be sent
To my enemy.

A father's response

I need him in the morning, before my breakfast
I need him in the evening, with my final thought.

When I cannot feed my family, he provides for us
When I overwhelmed by our enemy, he rises to defend us
When I am not capable, he steps in and is my aide
When I am lost, he knows the destination and guides us to it
When I am prone to take matters into my own hands, he places his
upon my shoulder
When I am being foolish, he corrects me.

So how can I have any response other than gratitude
And any posture other than that of service
And any daily worship other than that of love.

By the casket

The earth continues to turn
At a pace I cannot control
For if I could I would surely stop it.

But as morning turns to afternoon
All resilience, balm and wisdom
Is overcome by the dread only a parent can know.

Ungraceful time shows no mercy to me and does not relent
As friends, ritual and ceremony support my climb
My burden getting heavier minute by minute.

I wish time would stop and everyone would disappear and we
could continue
But the minute hand of the clock on the wall prises you out of my
hands
And takes you where I cannot follow.

Here standing by the casket I am hollowed out.
By a roughly hewn but wholly effective instrument
And find I do not have the strength or courage say farewell.

Descending from that hill
Empty, robbed and overwhelmed
I sense His closeness.

And as I lay my head on my pillow
Unable to orient myself with my thoughts
Afresh I hear the kind carol remind me

That the hopes and fears of all the years are met in thee tonight.

Love is not blind

Far out to sea where birds are rare
And hill and shore are never seen
No eye of man gives witness there
To mysteries held in blue and green.

A flash of scales from flank and fin
As soaked sun's rays tell secrets kept
Wet reflections grey and thin
As light descends to dark and depth.

No one but Maker sees this sight
And yet it still is orchestrated
Performance for His good delight
His world designed, by Him curated.

What else He sees that no eye catches?
That pleases him with hope fulfilled
Unseen echoes of image bearers
Placed in garden, commissioned , skilled.

All hidden kindness, restraint, forgiveness
His light reflects off creatures formed
Penetrates the depth and darkness
To where dimmed souls see hope reborn.

Man's accolades the ill formed measure
Of value viewed and silver screened
In contrast to the Makers pleasure
That loves the small, hidden, unseen.

Lord of the flies

You make your own annoying noise,
Yet are inadvertently playing someone else's beautiful song.
The virtuoso following the conductors baton.

You pride yourself in being king of this world,
Yet find yourself able to act only act as allowed.
Fleeing from the slightest wave of the resistant hand.

You move in manipulation and control
As a pawn in a mysterious game you do not comprehend.
Always a plaything on a leash for the children's entertainment.

You attach yourself with piercing hooks and cause pain,
Locating and landing on an open sore.
Revealing hurt and wound you signal the location and guide the
healing.

You are a servant to no-one,
But a slave to your own will,
Until the day when death is no more and there is no longer need
for your service.

When he speaks

The world is noisy and cluttered
But when He speaks Heaven is present
With so few words He cuts through to the heart of the heart of the
matter.

With language unencumbered by formality and loaded with
authority
The chattering court of my mind is silenced
And with every head bowed and knee bent
He answers my question before it is even formed upon my lips.

As the reverberation from his voice fades
And a stunned consciousness slowly rises to its feet,
The world is different.

A watershed moment

When all alone with pain too great to sustain
And when the road of hope seems far too short,
The opioid laden fang will embrace
Your very soul, and warm you
Holding you close, and never letting you leave
For you are now owned.

When all alone with pain too great to sustain
And the road of hope seems far too short
The quiet whispered prayer will be met with a warm embrace
Around your very soul, and enliven you
Drawing you close, and never leaving you
For you have always been loved

A peculiar voyage

Why are you so silent?
There are things I want to know and be certain of
And you know these things and make them certain.

There is no rule that you should include me in your confidence,
Though it would certainly give me courage for the journey if I
knew my way
Across this stormy sea.
Or in the doldrums, consuming my supplies, not moving.

I'm driven to confess I don't know where I'm going and I don't
know if I'm getting there.
The navigator won't let me see the charts
But gives directions at the right time.
And it can be seemingly ages between changes of course.

So I will take silence as 'keep going'
Though there are many who have kept going and wound up on the
rocks,
Who started well, and ended badly.
You did not prevent them from going their own way and running
aground.

So I strain my ears, with an aching focus to listen out for your
unvoiced whisper,
Afraid of missing the most quiet signal ,
Afraid of missing your guidance by the noise of my own hubris or
fear or self-pity

And so I learn, it is not your voice that trains me to listen to you,
But your silence.

Mutually inclusive

Torn between true love and honest duty
Years too short to let a single joy of life pass me by
And also to have it said I did not play my part
Until I realise I am whole, to love my duty, and to dutifully love.

Twinkle twinkle little star

Oh twinkling star that leads wise men to the anticipated child.
Easily hidden by cloud at night and by day's bright sun,
By mists of earth's passions that obscure you from my fickle gaze
Missing daily observations required to track constellation's
ordained position.
As I read the night sky to take my bearing.

I have no other guide yet become distracted
By a light that burns within rather than without,
Seeking by my own glow, a childish self
And disregarding your celestial pointing to the childlike other.
Whose ultimate Guide and Light could forever be my true north.

The day

Waking, soft and warm, I rub my eyes,
And with the birdsong greet the day.
Transitioning from dark imagination to the illuminated actual
As the sun changes from it's beautiful but solely orange glow to
include all the colors.
Landscapes and oceans and cities augmented with blues, greens
and white
A full, rich, balanced spectrum to sing His praises.

And so to work, hand to the wheel
Sweat and toil
Comradeship and laughter
Difficult and strain
Interjected with rest
Moving forward
Growing and expending
Until completion

The joy of being still in a short time of solitude,
The pacing of preparing the evening meal
The time to discuss matters of the day,
Of unpacking and reframing and coaching my thoughts and those
of others wanting to talk and listen.
And down again, for story time
By the glowing screen or paper narration.
Until it's time for farewells
And heavy eyes force my entirety to leave this day behind.

Appealing

Please

Please let go
Of all you carry
Burdens too heavy have shaped your back
Learn to walk upright in hand
With Jesus on life's sweet short track.

Please release
The tethered harpoon
You have embedded in your foes flank
Unclench the hands that hold rope tightly
Forgive, release and don't look back.

Please liberate
The slaves you hold
Controlled to serve your egos fear
Grant their freedom, give them blessing
Help them flourish, hold them dear.

Please embrace
Your Friend's great kindness
Enjoy his keen interest in you
Allow compassion, cleansing, closeness
Out with the old, in with the new

Retirement planning

"You can't take it with you"
Wise words concerning death's great financial filter.
If your heart is in this world
your treasures will also be here, safe and secure
Stuck on this side of the grave.

So choose Heaven's royal courage
Invest in His here and now kingdom
If your heart is in His ongoing creation
You'll receive an eternal pension
Paid out on both sides of the grave.

Heaven breaks through

Hands raised high like starling chicks
Demanding food with crass refrain,
"Breakthrough, breakthrough" rings loud insistence
"Fall afresh and entertain."

Prayer is answered and grace is given
Yet not to chicks in nested home,
But those on ground, fallen and broken
Unnoticed, hopeless and alone.

Breakthrough indeed their pain and sorrow
Their lonely terror, grief and shame,
Keep them safe and feed their hunger
Breakthrough their label, know their name.

ABOUT THE AUTHOR

Richard grew up in the Southwest of England, moving to New Zealand when he was 16 where he now lives with his wife and 3 children.

With a background in law, computer science and business, his vocation has seen him work in Australia, England, New Zealand and Saudi Arabia, and it is these wildly different experiences and learnings that have, in the addition to the study of scriptures, informed his Christian faith, the reflections of which are now found in this small, initial collection of poems, that he stumbled across in the desert.

Printed in Great Britain
by Amazon

34680862R00037